Affairs of the Heart

by

Renee Cabrera

authorHOUSE®

AuthorHouse™
1663 Liberty Drive, Suite 200
Bloomington, IN 47403
www.authorhouse.com
Phone: 1-800-839-8640

First published by AuthorHouse 11/13/2008

ISBN: 978-1-4389-1292-9 (sc)

Printed in the United States of America
Bloomington, Indiana

This book is printed on acid-free paper.

This book is dedicated to my son, Nikolaus.

These words, feelings and experiences
have made me who I am today......

<u>THE MOM!</u>

Preface

The best two phrases I've ever heard someone speak are; "It's not who you are but what you do that defines you" and "We fall so we can learn to pick ourselves up".

I've never believed such truer words. I've always thought I was a good person; raised right, polite, conscientious and courteous, but making others FEEL good was more important and learning from my mistakes was key.

These poems helped me work and think thru my thoughts, feelings and actions.

If just one person understands, relates and learns from my words and experiences then I am truly STRONG AND DEFINED.

When life's got you down and you're feeling a bit blue;
Just remember I'm here as a friend for you.

When you find yourself sad and losing that smile;
Just give me and call and we'll talk for a while.

When you've come to the point where you've done all you can do;
Just never give up; I'll be there for you.

There are many gifts that life can bring;
But a wonderful family is everything.

Through ups and downs, good and bad;
You remember something you've always had.

That gift of love and togetherness;
Because a family is where the heart is.

We share laughter
We share fun
But we hold secrets from everyone.

I see you sad
You see me cry
Yet we feel better before we say good bye.

I long for him
You long for her
Though only 'WE' are there for each other.

When you need a hug
I'm always here
If I need a hug, you're always there.

We talk as friends
We fight as family
But to break us up would devastate me.

My ears are listening
My shoulder is there
My heart is warm because I care.

So when you need me or not
A message you'll send
Because I'll do anything at all for my special 'Boy' friend.

Happy Birthday to
The man of my life;
You filled my heart when you made me your wife.

Thru the years
We've had our share;
Of good and bad with some to spare.

But I wouldn't change a thing you see;
Because you, my love
Mean the world to me.

Just a blink was all it took;
And you jumped out of a fairy tale book.

You changed my views of love and fun;
You showed me I could believe in someone.

You're a million in one and you care about me too;
That's why I'm so much in love with you.

Kiss me, Caress me and hug me tight;
Make a promise to me on this starry night.

As I close my eyes to that shooting star;
And wish that our hearts will never be far.

I'll wish of laughter no sorrow or pain;
I'll wish that together our lives will remain.

I'll wish for your hand, always in mine;
And wish for strength even thru bad times.

But my greatest wish is not afar;
Because 'YOU' were my wish upon a star.

Being a boss is not always easy
It takes a special kind.

But when we need a personal friend
You always find the time.

Your strong hand in business
Makes us get the job done.

Yet your kind understanding and helpful touch
Can compare to none.

So let me take this time to reminisce about all that we've been thru
And extend a very warm and friendly "Thanks" for being you.

$\mathcal{M}$arriage is a challenge many dare to take;
It's a commitment for life that a couple will make.

You've taken that step to live life as one;
And share your experiences, some boring some fun.

You'll go through changes in body and mind;
Solutions and compromises together you'll find.

There will be those times of heartache and despair;
But they won't compete with the happy ones you'll share.

And as the years go on and your souls unite;
As husband and wife you'll share a special insight.

You're happiness and sorrow will be noticed as the same;
Because you love one another will be the blame.

So the vow you took "til death do us part";
Is an eternal bond shared in the heart.

It means more than just "together for life";
Because you rise above as husband and wife.

*Y*ou came to me like a gift from the sky;
How I got so lucky, I'll never know why.

Your gentle kindness came like a shock;
It all went so fast, I just couldn't yell stop.

It's not like I wanted to, don't get me wrong;
It's just people like you hardly ever come along.

You're so nice to me, I just can't understand;
In need or not your hold out your hand.

But remember that if you ever need me;
Just call once and I'll come running....you'll see.

$\mathcal{I}$ build this wall so no one will get near;
For I know that I will be safe in here.

I've lost all faith; I've lost all trust;
To put it in someone is simply unjust.

How could jealousy be so strong?
To break up something that could last so long?

It's hard to find a friend in which we develop trust;
But in a world like this, one simply must.

And when one finds this trust, watch out for peers;
They can turn this trust into your greatest fear.

It's hard for me to express my feelings
And tell you how I care.

All I can do is show you
Because I love you being there.

Your kisses are soft
Your touch is kind

How else can I say
Through good and bad;
I love you anyway

To write a poem is all I can do;
To express my feelings to the world and you.

To express myself in person is hard for me;
But give me a pen and I'll write a masterpiece.

I can write good and bad, love and hate;
Because writing is my only way to communicate.

Don't misunderstand, I love to talk and listen;
But to know my feelings just watch my pen glisten.

The arguments we have are a message from above
Someone's trying to tell us
They're arguments of love.

When we argue, it's not for the worst
We're just trying to tell each other
"I love you" first.

So please don't forget
The message from above
Trying to explain our arguments of love.

You tell me you love me
I know it's true
And in so many ways, I love you too.

Sometimes we part, but it's never forever
For we both know in time
We'll soon be together.

I haven't spent any holidays with you
I know that you
Have a family too.

But when I have you
It's better than the rest
My time spent with you is simply the best.

I love you very dearly
I guess you just don't understand
That every time I talk to you, you could use that 'one' sentence to
  end.

I know it's not that easy to do
Your ways are just so different
But maybe it's the difference that makes me love you.

You've helped me so much
You gave me a shove when I wanted to give up
Surely that's why our love won't stop.

I love you so much
I hope we don't part
Everything I say to you comes straight from the heart.

All the presents you give are special you see
But the best gift of all is the one you've given me.

So don't get down if you hear me cry
It's the love you've given me, if you're wondering why.

And when I get mad it's only because I care
For if I lost you now, I'd die my worst dare.

So you didn't have an awesome game
Just keep your chin up, things always change.

You didn't make a wonderful play
You can't always expect a perfect day.

It wasn't your night but you gave what you had
I knew how you felt and I couldn't help but feel sad.

As you walked to the plate, my heart filled with fear
The outcome really hurt you, your eyes filled with tears.

I was sad to see the tears in your eye
I saw them before when you said good bye.

But it's ok, I'm glad they were there
It proved to me that you deeply care.

I wish I could help since you're feeling so blue
Just know the hug was for real and my sincerity too.

Love comes to the unexpected
Especially those who seem to neglect it.

Those who look find nothing to gain
Besides the fact of heartache and pain.

Yet looking is fun but for what it's worth
Be patient and safe to avoid all the hurt.

$\mathcal{L}$ife is a place for change and reason
A chance for exposure to the world and its seasons.

A time to learn what there is to teach
Grasping for more with perfection in reach.

The rise of the sun at the dawn of the day
Keeping a smile though times are gray.

Taking the time to say a prayer
For the beauty of life God wanted to share.

Two wonderful years of love and joy
Shared in the world by a girl and a boy.

So much in love yet so far apart
Held together by a bonded heart.

And then it shattered like a heart of glass
If only the distance hadn't taken the past.

For a year and a half there was no fate
They blinded their love with a silent hate.

But then one day as she wandered around
A small little office was where she was found.

Lifting her head she looked in his eyes
So much precious time had passed them by.

They walked on the beach and reminisced in the sand
He later sealed their love and asked for her hand.

$\mathscr{A}$ father is someone who's always there
To give that special loving care.

He helps you out when you're in a bind
And backs you up when you've fallen behind.

He shares his wisdom to help you grow
Yet doesn't deny what you already know.

Now as an adult you look in the past
To those childhood memories that last and last.

Though many were good and some were bad
Who was always there?
Your father – your Dad.

$\mathcal{T}$here are so many things that I'd like to say
But if I do you might walk away.

We were the best of friends and we only get closer
How were we to know that something special would flower.

What we want now is different than before; at least that's how it
    seems
Please try and understand, I want you to know what I mean.

I'm afraid of losing our friendship too
But I realize it's still here after what we've gone thru.

We know what we want to do but somehow we just can't
I guess it's because we made another commitment.

Me with him and you with her is what they want to see
It hurts so bad within my heart, together is what we should be.

I won't give up, I'll keep holding on until the time is right
Because the bond we have makes the grip so tight.

But there is one thing that I have not said and I know that I have
    to
Because it would hurt me more to walk away since I've fallen so
    deeply for you.

On the month of December, year 92;
I gave birth to a boy, that child was you.

You were just what I needed, my life needed change;
From that point on nothing would be the same.

I made some choices that turned out bad;
But you gave me the strength I never knew I had.

We have a bond with honesty and truth,
And I'm sad that by baby's out growing his youth.

But I'll watch you grow older and be proud of your life;
You'll be a great man and you'll have a great wife.

Thru ups and downs, I had finally learned;
That only your choices can make your life turn.

I fell in a hole then climbed my way out;
I opened my eyes to what life was about.

My life got better; my son was growing strong;
Then by the grace of God, you came along.

Of all the things I was working to fix;
I didn't expect you to fit in the mix.

But we got so attached so quickly and fast;
It just felt so right that we were meant to last.

In no time at all we were saying "I do";
And everyday since I fall more in love with you.

Life is a story book, a journey to take;
But life can only be what you make.

Your choices are yours, they pave the way;
Of what your life will be each day.

Be honest and open, caring and free;
When you lose your direction just call to me.

What else can I do but feel so sad,
All I think about is the specialness we had.

It was taken away by someone who doesn't matter;
SHE made all of our happiness shatter.

She'll do anything to keep you away from me,
It's eating my heart but I fear to let you see.

How can she do that? Why does she dare?
Is it really so wrong to show you I care?

She's told you lies, I've heard what she's said;
I keep going over and over them in my head.

What evil is inside her? Is loving you so wrong?
I guess our growing friendship made her jealousy strong.

Now the game is over and I have lost;
Being in it, my feelings have been tossed.

Whenever you need me I'll always be here;
You'll see how I feel in one single tear.

I feel so hurt she says she's won;
But what else can I do, what's done is done.

"Let's not make it a discussion", is what you say;
Whenever things aren't going your way.

And when I persist you have nothing to say;
Then we don't talk for the rest of the day.

You don't care what I feel or what's in my heart;
This is something that tears me apart.

My attitude and mood are not the seed;
It occurs because I feel I'm not what you need.

I know I lack in the affection part;
But I thought couples worked together to combine at the heart.

Learning and loving as one was the vow;
That used to be us but it isn't now.

You've known me for years and I've tried to change;
But you, my dear, have stayed the same.

And I love you for you, so how can it be;
That you're always unhappy and disappointed with me?

We need to start now to communicate;
Or we'll wake up one day for it to be too late.

I support you in all that you do and you say;
I hope someday you could treat me that way.

You think I'm naïve and not very bright;
Just open your mind and surprise you I might.

I'm not asking for romance, it's not your style;
Just show me you'd go that last extra mile.

To explain where I'm coming from, the phrase I most find;
'Taken for granted' is what comes to mind.

$\mathcal{I}$t all begins with an amazing love;
Then a seed is planted by a single white dove.

There's a heaven inside you but a 9 month wait;
To see the creation you've made could come early or late.

Then one day you cry and shout;
It's your child-to-be ready to come out.

Is it too much to bare? All the pushing and pain?
Maybe at times but imagine the gain.

And on that last push, you reach down to touch;
The head of the child you'll love so much.

As you bring your child close your heart fills with joy;
To know you've created a little Baby Boy!

You go to sleep-he's there;
You awake-he's there;
You're happy-he's there;
You cry-he's there;
Who else could this be but your Teddy Bear.

He's so cuddly and cute with open arms;
He keeps you safe when you feel harm.

When you do something good and there's no one around;
Just simply tell the teddy bear you found.

The smile on his face fulfills your excitement;
Of telling someone of your accomplishment.

Your teddy is your true best friend;
Because no matter what they always understand.

Your teddy is the one who'll never let you down;
Because in times of the heart, he's always around.

Happiness is...........

The moon in the dark
The sun in the day
The stars in the night
A child who prays

The fish in the ocean
The birds in the trees
The sky of blue
And the grass of green

The joy of life
The understanding of death
A thank you to God
For every breath

A special friend
A kind hug
A gentle kiss
Someone to snug

But most of all it's a gift to give
Because that's the meaning of what happiness is.

$\mathcal{A}$ friend once told me that life was a game;
So no matter what was going on I shouldn't take the blame.

If life is a game that everyone plays;
Then no wonder why friendships don't stay.

Why do feelings have to be toyed?
Shouldn't life be something to enjoy?

People take advantage of something so grand;
Although the few who don't are too minimal to take a stand.

When it's too late that's when people realize;
The life they should have recognized.

And the people they hurt will still be there;
The ones from before won't even show care.

So I'll keep my opinion of how life should be;
For the ones who don't notice now will someday look back to me.

I'm glad I met this friend of mine;
He helps me remember that everything will be fine.

Up and down, round and round;
Like a yo-yo is the relationship we've found.

The contradictions of actions and words;
Makes the confusion of moving away or toward.

Similar to a child caught up in play;
With the thought that he may have to leave for the day.

Though in his departure his heart feels bright;
To return to the same he knew someday he might.

But with this knowledge, his face still frowned;
For it was a walk in the park until the sun went down.

5 years have passed, you don't know how I've grown;
But I can still remember the memories I've known.

I had too much pride to speak from my heart;
Because I was selfish it tore us apart.

I understood you and you cared about me;
So thanks to "them" we are where we should be.

Times always were good, they rarely got bad;
Not understanding YOU is what made me sad.

But that's all changed; I'm willing to try;
Because after all this time I can't let you pass by.

Through all this time, what's left to say?
My how time has slipped away.

Do you know how special you are?
As I watch over you from near and afar.

And as I watch, I remember in time;
All the memories that are yours and mine.

You've grown so much in heart and soul; there is no more to do;
As I feel love in my heart and tears in my eyes, because I've
    watched your dreams come true.

$\mathcal{I}$t seems so strange that there can be;
Something as wonderful as you and me.

We're with one another thru good and bad;
Just think of all the fun we have.

But what are we? There is no name;
We both just hope things stay the same.

We take our walks; we have our talks and especially have our fun;
But we keep this secret in our hearts until confession day has come.

I feel for him, you feel for her but still it's not the same;
Our hearts are aching for you and me, all this hiding is a game.

Why did it happen? What possessed us to show the way we feel?
Something tells me that God did it to prove to us what is real.

Why are we so afraid to live this dream which God made us create;
Maybe now he's testing our strength because good things always wait.

So someday soon things will uncover and feelings will strengthen
   or end;
But we secretly know what God wants and that's the feelings
   toward a best friend.

A seed was planted in good soil long ago;
Who would have known that beauty would grow?

It had velvet pedals and also had thorns;
Right through the skin could they have torn.

But in its development the thorns were weak and there were only
the pedals of the rose;
How could they have strengthened so hard and so fast? Only one
person knows.

Slowly the pedals fell to the ground and the thorns turned weak again;
The flower was dying in more ways than one and never to re-begin.

Although the grower tried so hard to bring life back to the rose;
Why wouldn't water and new soil help? Only that same person knows.

So many questions, so little answers the grower felt defeat;
But then she realized with her heart that beauty is only skin deep.

It's a tug of war inside my heart;
The feelings I have are tearing me apart.

Like hide and seek it's just a game;
We hide; they seek, could we be afraid of change?

But my fuse is short, I'm about to explode;
I'm in love with you and I will let them know.

You push me away but it can't go on;
For I know you too well and your feelings are strong.

We built a love so young at heart;
For years we loved though we were apart.

But while you were gone they gave me a shove;
Tearing me away from our true love.

I thought I'd survive and get thru the time;
And find another love to be mine.

But it wasn't the same I kept it inside;
I thought it'd get better if I just let it slide.

Everyone was happy while I fell apart;
There was a large empty hole deep in my heart.

Then one day we rebuilt anew;
The love we had between me and you.

And this time I promise "until death do us part"
That I'll follow my instincts and be guided by my heart.

"What goes around comes around" is always what they say;
Well here I am with you again in a similar sort of way.

We parted once to live our lives and go out on our own;
To only realize there's nothing wonderful about always being alone.

We can learn together of this world of ours and all its ups and downs;
Because "what goes around comes around" may not always come
    back around.

$\mathcal{I}$t doesn't hurt now because I am safe;
I have the security, I know the place.

It's in your arms right by your side;
You give me the strength so I will not hide.

Your arms get loose now you hold my hand;
But by your side is where I stand.

You see fear in my eyes so you pull me back;
The tears in my eyes are beginning to stack.

Waving good bye, I lose you in sight;
I keep holding on while the plane is in flight.

I must let go; now the pain has begun;
We're 2 apart but our hearts are one.

$\mathcal{I}$ open my eyes and there he is, he's sleeping in my bed;
A single tear falls from my eyes in away it never did.

It feels so good to have him here from evening until day;
I hope to God that every time would always be this way.

But this evening came and he decided he wanted to go home instead;
So I let him go thinking it would be fine yet I now can't sleep in this bed.

The best of friends we'll always be;
It'll be that way until eternity.

When you walked into my life I felt in my heart;
Nothing could ever tear us apart.

But something is different, we aren't as close;
We've both grown up is what I suppose.

Just remember my friend that I'm always here;
Whether it be far or near.

I'll come to you with open arms;
No questions asked, I'll protect you from harm.

We'll walk together hand in hand;
And that's how it will be until the end.

The time has come to say good bye;
On the outside we're happy on the inside we cry.

You'll go your way, I'll go mine;
And in the long run everything will be fine.

We'll forget the bad and remember the good;
Just as we always knew we could.

You have one fault which you cannot deny;
You always hide your feelings inside.

Someday you'll find someone to share them with;
Just don't be afraid, hold on to your strength.

You're a special guy; I see it in you;
So if you put your mind to it there's nothing you can't do.

You'll do great in baseball but don't forget school;
As soon as you slack off you'll be playing the fool.

I know you can do it though it's going to be hell;
Just remember one thing, do it for yourself.

$\mathcal{I}$t's been so long since our time together;
The memories we hold are lasting forever.

The moments we shared as a family and friends;
Have remained in our hearts for they shall never end.

So in this time which we reunite;
We'll reminisce on the times we miss.

The love of old friends has made us strong;
For we know in our hearts where our souls belong.

So let's take this time to say a prayer;
With hope that these friendships will always be there.

We were divorced with a child to tend;
Nothing was cordial, it was a bitter end.

He brought her in and made her his wife;
Now she was part of my little boy's life.

But a child herself, what did she know;
How could she help my child grow?

She tried to connect and would not fall;
Pushing thru my emotional wall.

She would bridge the gap and hold on tight;
Being the middle-man in every fight.

She had a good heart; my son loved her so;
She gave me respect though I never let it show.

Now she's in my shoes, for she was next;
She too became a single-mom ex.

But even after their marital end;
His ex is now and always my friend.

$\mathcal{L}$ife is like baseball, three strikes you're out;
Friendship's no different, more painful no doubt.

Especially to those who don't have a clue;
You realize your friend's attack is on you.

It was building for years but you couldn't see;
In your 'loyalty to friendship' you were naïve.

Every time, you forgave and forgot;
Never realizing a 'friend' she was not.

Now the game is over, again, painful no doubt;
But sometimes it's safer just to get out.

*L*ast night I cried myself to sleep;
The hurt I was holding came from so very deep.

I wouldn't let go, I kept it inside;
It hurts so badly, I felt I would die.

The ones whom I love are slipping away;
I fear I'll wake up and they'll be all gone one day.

But why couldn't I talk and tell you these things;
I suppose I was afraid of the outcome it'd bring.

The closer you get toward my heart;
The more I keep pushing us apart.

As I cried over them, I cried over you;
With fear that I may be losing you too.

What could be happening?
What's going on?
We haven't laughed and talked for so long.

I know it's me and the things I hide;
It would kill me to lose you because of my pride.

Believe me I'm trying but what can I do?
I only want things to be happy for you.

It makes me so happy to do your tasks;
Anything you want, I'll do it just ask.

I don't want anything but a simple hug and kiss;
In a room full of people it's you that I miss.

How much else could you possibly be?
You already mean the world to me.

I'd leave my friend; I'd leave a date;
Just so 'you' wouldn't have to wait.

Just want you to know to never give up;
100% is how I'll back you up.

You are wonderful, you'll be great;
So having you near me is worth the wait.

There's a hole in my life
There's a tear in my heart;
They are there because we are so far apart.

There is no happiness
There are no chimes
Because you are gone for months at a time.

But I do hear bells
I see girls in white
For when we're together, we are a beautiful sight.

You're a wonderful ball player so have no fear;
You'll get your wish to get out of here.

Don't doubt your ability; don't doubt your skill;
You'll go very far, I know you will.

Do for yourself not what others expect;
But never give up, you'll lose my respect.

I've heard you talk; I've shared your dream;
So seeing you out there means everything to me.

I saw you play here; I'll see you play there;
I'll follow your dream with you everywhere.

Now you know how much it means to me too;
But most of all remember, I'll be here for you.

You're different
You're special
You're one of a kind
You're the kind of thought that sticks in my mind.

I fell for you because of fate;
Because good things come to those who wait.

I have confidence in you I cannot control;
You're fulfilling a dream that you want to uphold.

Baseball's your life
It's in your heart
It means so much that it tore us apart.

But I understand now you can only have one;
Me or 'it', the choice is done.

I only want what's best for you;
 And in enough time my day will come too.

So I stand behind you and back you up;
100% so you'll never stop.

I can't express enough how much I care;
Just want you to know that I'll always be there.

And if you ever need me don't hesitate;
Because good things come to those who wait.

When we split up I felt my heart break;
But to get you back I could only but wait.

On your way back you sort of got lost;
And in the confusion my feelings got tossed.

A wall was built by family and friends;
No one wanted us together again.

Not them
Not you
And sometimes not me
For it wouldn't be the same as it used to be.

Although I'll admit that I still feel the pain;
At times when I think of 'US' again.

But your friendship means more to me right now;
If I could get it back please tell me how.

$\mathscr{I}$ don't know what you think about me
To you it may not matter;
But hearing you say you care about me fills my heart with flatter.

I know you have some doubts about me
I have them too about you
But what you really can't understand is that I honestly care about you.

What a beautiful sight shooting across the sky
How did it happen?
The question is why?

A shooting star with sparkle and shine;
I wish I could hold that star to be mine.

It makes us feel special as though no one else had known;
About the beautiful glow which the star had shown.

But how many demands could such beauty take;
A wish from the star did each of us make.

Who wished for the star?
The glitter goes away;
With hope of seeing it again someday.

There once was a guy I loved so much;
He took me places, gave me presents and such.

Well he smiled and gave me a kiss on the cheek;
Then said he'd be back in just a short week.

The day he came back he played our song;
He let me to believe we were going on strong.

He said he loved me
I believed him so
We broke up just a short while ago.

$\mathcal{I}$ look to the night
It's calling to me
The moon say "come on"
The stars say "please".

I want to so much
But I'm being held back
An unknown force is on attack.

"Let me go to where it's beautiful and free"
"In the night is where I long to be"

It's simply no use and the night goes away
"Please don't go I want you to stay"

As the sun peaks up to reach its height
I open my eyes and he's holding me tight.

$\mathcal{T}$he perfect male has qualities that every woman wants and needs:

He's handsome, smart, clean cut and neat;
He walks to a cute and uppity beat.

His smile is warm, his touch is kind;
He's built to the perfection you see in your mind.

He talks so fluent you gaze in his eyes;
You're crying at the fact that he says good-bye.

So this is the male women want on hand;
Well good luck to them, I'm describing 'My man'

Once in a lifetime someone comes along
To stand by your side and make you feel strong!

They hold your hand thru good times and bad;
Extending open arms at times when you're sad.

You lean on them and they lean on you;
Because there comes a time when you're 1 not 2.

So you see, love is a lesson that can not be taught;
You just know it happened when you finish their thoughts.

And when there are obstacles-people, places and things;
You tighten your bond with the symbol of a ring.

Now give me your hand as I've given you mine;
Because 'You & Me' come once in a lifetime.

He has teaching to guide thru good and bad;
Strength to protect in times happy and sad.

Arms to caress a sleepless fright;
Kisses warm for the cold of the night.

He was sent by God, an angel with wings;
No harm shall come, the future he's seen.

No more evil, no more fear;
Safety falls when he is near.

Angel of God this prince of love;
He was sent to me from heaven above.

I'll love him til death though at death not us part;
Marriage is eternal when straight from the heart.

A breath of fresh air as it glows from beneath;
Rising to its harmonious peak.

Dazzling the day and the world as a whole;
Sanctifying the heart and soul.

Giving us energy to go that last mile;
What could it be but the beauty of a smile.

Friends forever is what I believe;
But I've always known that I was naïve.

But this one was different; she didn't stab me in the back;
She looked me in the eye with every attack.

The trust I bestowed, the faith I had;
The malice from her makes me so sad.

I pity her for what she could do to a friend;
But I know I'm better off, I win in the end.

The sun comes up
The sun goes down
But my life's always bright when you're around.

Your warm smile
Your gentle hug
Makes my heart feel safe and snug.

The gradual progress of our friendship is strong;
I have a feeling it'll last very long.

The emotions I have are all so new;
Simply because I care about you.

We share so much, the laughter and pain;
I really love the relationship we've gained.

I'll pick you up if you should fall;
Because in a friendship like ours, love conquers all.

Today was the worst which I ever had;
To watch you walk away only made me feel sad.

I couldn't do anything without you here;
I couldn't go anywhere without you near.

I was hurting so bad but what else could I do;
Things only went well when I was with you.

For better
For worse
Things always work out.

In good
In bad
Have no fear or no doubt.

Follow your heart
Do what you feel
Things won't fall apart
All good things will heal.

The guy I date is good to me;
We've gone places I've only dreamt to be.

Sometimes our evening turn out bad;
But what is special is the togetherness we have.

At times we like to go out with our friends,
At times we like to be alone.

But no matter how close or how far apart;
We should never forget we're in one another's heart.

$\mathcal{W}$e hold a hidden secret which no one else can know;
So only with each other can we let our feelings show.

I don't think this secret can come to an end;
We get along so well as lovers and as friends.

It seems so very strange because people always say;
To have 2 in 1 like us, the relationship won't stay.

We love each others company and we always have our fun;
So to hold our feelings back could no longer be done.

Someday the time will come to 'tell', as distant as it seems;
To show everyone what's been going on inside our secret dream.

But as for now the secret will hold for it's what we have to do;
It's just so hard to stand in a crowd and hide my feelings about
    you.

$\mathcal{I}$ want to say sorry about the attacks;
But it's the only way to get my strength back.

I have to be tough and only you know why;
It's simply the fact I've been hurt so many times.

Having you near makes it all seem OK;
Since in the past, you have stayed.

You know it's not personal; I love you so much;
As a brother, a boyfriend, a best friend and such.

So please understand all that I do;
For someday I'll be strong especially for you.

$\mathcal{I}$ love our friendship, please let it stay;
We get along so well in a special sort of way.

We write, talk, and go out to eat;
A friendship like this I could never repeat.

If I'm in need or not you're always there;
Outsiders feel that our friendship's unfair.

They make accusations spread rumors and such;
They simply don't value a friendship that much.

But I value ours and all that we do;
And most of all I love my friend, that's you.

The first time I saw you, you were just another view;
But the day that we met I saw it was you.

The one to take care of me
To worry over me
To love me
Things that, I too, could do for you.

Many times in my dreams I would try to see;
That one mysterious face that actually cared about me.

What you say and do to me is like my dreams have come true;
For I see in my dreams that face has been you.

By fate we've come together, our love could not be dissolved;
You're the one I want to be with, with you my mysteries are solved.

You called, asked me out for Friday night;
I accepted willingly but my stomach felt fright.

I really liked you and wanted nothing to go wrong;
So just thinking of you made my encouragement strong.

We left at eight, a movie we caught;
At first I was nervous, we didn't really talk.

But during the movie our hands embraced;
Being with you just made me feel safe.

When I came home I was happy to see;
The sparkle in your eye after you kissed me.

I knew you then
I know you now
You slipped away then and I don't know how.

Now that I've had you I can't let you go;
The thought of 'US' makes my happiness flow.

We have understandings
We have our fun
To tear us apart simply shouldn't be done.

I understand the difficulty for you to trust;
Please believe in me, you honestly must.

I have a dream when I'm with you;
It's making love under the moon.

Our intimate moments mean so much;
Even down to your simplest touch.

Each of us go out on dates;
But in time of need there won't be wait.

I don't know what else to say to you;
Except I'll always be in love with you.

When I first saw you we exchanged "hellos";
The next time I saw you we rubbed elbows.

I saw you again near the end of the day;
You asked for my number, I gave it not knowing what to say.

You called me that night, I nearly died;
Talking to you makes me tingle inside.

I now understand the cliché 'love at first sight';
Whoever said it well….they were right.

As children we'd fight, then fake to make-up;
As youths we'd argue, then negotiate our stuff.

As teens we parted and thought it'd be great;
To be away from each other was a long wanted wait.

Though something had changed, I didn't know what;
An 'I miss you' feeling came from the gut.

And the day finally came that I saw it so clearly;
My darling brother, "I love you dearly".

$\mathcal{A}$ heart of stone will always work
When a heart of warmth has gotten you hurt.

I'll keep my chin up and hold my head high
For another guy will soon pass by.

But if he gets too close I'll push away
Behind an invisible wall is where I'll stay.

I'll learn to deal with rejection and pain
And my self esteem I'll never regain.

Because life is filled with ups and downs
Only when a guy is around.

My hands are cold, my heart is stone
Just because of the guys I've known.

$\mathcal{M}$om and Dad,

I get angry sometimes for you correcting me
And I get angry also for the things you DON'T see.

I get furious when you tell me
The guy I like is no good for me.

And when you tell me sometimes what I'm wearing looks bad
You really don't see that it makes me feel sad.

I only want you to be proud of me
But still you seem to find my bad qualities.

You upset me for things you do and say
But I know you love me anyway.

And as I grow older I finally see
You only want what's best for me.

You're special mom and dad
Please never go away
I love you a lot

Your daughter, Renee

Printed in the United States
129939LV00002B/142/P